ISBN 978-0-86037-37-4

MUSLIM CHILDREN'S LIBRARY
General Editors: Khurram Murad and Mushuq Ally

THE KINGDOM OF JUSTICE
Author: Khurram Murad
Illustrations: Bookmatrix
Cover Design: Nasir Cadir
Coordinator: Anwar Cara
Editing: Mardijah A. Tarantino

These stories are about the Prophet and his Companions and, though woven around authentic ahadith, should only be regarded as stories.

Published by

THE ISLAMIC FOUNDATION,
Markfield Conference Centre,
Ratby Lane, Markfield,
Leicestershire, LE67 9SY, United Kingdom
Website: www.islamic-foundation.org.uk

QURAN HOUSE, P.O. Box 30611, Nairobi, Kenya

P.M.B. 3193, Kano, Nigeria

All enquiries to:
Kube Publishing
Tel: +44(0)1530 249230, Fax +44(0)1530 249656
Email: info@kubepublishing.com
www.kubepublishing.com

A catalogue record of this book is available from British Library

The KINGDOM of JUSTICE

Stories from the Life of Umar

Khurram Murad

THE ISLAMIC FOUNDATION

MUSLIM CHILDREN'S LIBRARY

An Introduction.

Here is a new series of books, but with a difference, for children of all ages. Published by the Islamic Foundation, books in the Muslim Children's Library have been produced to provide young people with something they cannot perhaps find anywhere else.

Most of today's children's books aim only to entertain and inform or to teach some necessary skills, but not to develop the inner and moral resources. Entertainment and skills by themselves impart nothing of value to life unless a child is also helped to discover deeper meaning in himself and the world around him. Yet there is no place in them for God, Who alone gives meaning to life and the universe, nor for the Divine Guidance brought by His prophets, following which can alone ensure an integrated development of the total personality.

Such books, in fact, rob young people of access to true knowledge. They give them no unchanging standards of right and wrong, nor any incentives to live by what is right and refrain from what is wrong. The result is that all too often the young enter adult life in a state of social alienation and bewilderment, unable to cope with the seemingly unlimited choices of the world around them. The situation is especially devastating for the Muslim child as he may grow up cut off from his culture and values.

The Muslim Children's Library aspires to remedy this deficiency by showing children the deeper meaning of life and the world around them by pointing them along paths leading to an integrated development of all aspects of their personality; by helping to give them the capacity to cope with the complexities of their world, both personal and social; by opening vistas into a world extending far beyond this life; and, to a Muslim child especially, by providing a fresh and strong faith, a dynamic commitment, an indelible sense of identity, a throbbing yearning and an urge to struggle, all rooted in Islam. The books aim to help a child anchor his development on the rock of divine guidance, and to understand himself and relate to himself and others in just and meaningful ways. They relate directly to his soul and intellect, to his emotions and imagination, to his motives and desires, to his anxieties and hopes — indeed, to every aspect of his fragile, but potentially rich personality. At the same time it is recognised that for a book to hold a child's attention, he must enjoy reading it; it should therefore arouse his curiosity and entertain him as well. The style, the language, the illustrations and the production of the books are all geared to this goal. They provide moral education, but not through sermons or ethical abstractions.

Although these books are based entirely on Islamic teachings and the vast Muslim heritage, they should be of equal interest and value to all children, whatever their country or creed; for Islam is a universal religion, the natural path.

Adults, too, may find much of use in them. In particular, Muslim parents and teachers will find that they provide what they have for so long been so badly needing. The books will include texts on the Qur'ān, the *Sunnah* and other basic sources and teachings of Islam, as well as history, stories and anecdotes for supplementary reading.

We invite parents and teachers to use these books in homes and classrooms, at breakfast tables and bedside and encourage children to derive maximum benefit from them. At the same time their greatly valued observations and suggestions are highly welcome. To the young reader we say: you hold in your hands books which may be entirely different from those you have been reading till now, but we sincerely hope you will enjoy them; try, through these books, to understand youself, your life, your experiences and the universe around you. They will open before your eyes new paths and models in life that you will be curious to explore and find exciting and rewarding to follow.

May God be with you forever. May Allah bless with His mercy and acceptance our humble contribution to the urgent and gigantic task of producing books for a new generation of people, a task which we have undertaken in all humility and hope.

Khurram Jah Murad
Director General

8

Contents

1

Fatima, too would have been punished

There was once a woman who lived in Makka. She belonged to a respected and noble family from the tribe of Makhzoom. She had committed a theft, and was faced, as a result, with the punishment of having her hand cut off. Her name was Fatima — the same name as the Prophet's (Peace and Blessings be upon him)* daughter. This incident happened in Makka, immediately after the city had surrendered to the Blessed Prophet. Many, many people had embraced Islam by then but they were not yet very good Muslims nor had they adjusted to the new standards of Islamic justice, which required that all Muslims, of noble or low birth, be treated in like manner for whatever crimes they committed.

---

*Muslims are required to invoke Allah's blessings and peace upon the Prophet whenever his name is mentioned.

Before Islam, the law would have been different for people like these of high birth than for those of low birth. They were very unhappy that a lady of high rank belonging to them, should be punished at all. 'How can it be so! Cannot there be some way to save her?' The grumbling grew more and more. But the question was how to convince the Blessed Prophet to release Fatima from punishment. They knew that it would be useless for them to ask him for leniency in a punishment ordained by God. After much deliberation they decided to seek the help of Usama, the son of Zayd.

Zayd, as you will remember, was the Blessed Prophet's servant, his adopted son, and one of the first four to believe in his message. The Blessed Prophet, naturally, loved Usama as he did Zayd, and for this reason the family from Makhzoom thought that perhaps if Usama had a quiet word with the Prophet, Fatima would be forgiven. Usama, at the time, was still a young lad. A young lad is usually high-spirited and eager to prove himself and play an important role in the eyes of his elders. He feels very elated when anyone, let alone a noble family of the Makhzoom, comes to him for help.

'Usama', they said, 'surely you can understand our plight. Look at Fatima, what an innocent girl she is. Should she be punished like a common thief? How could she have guessed that such a small mistake would cost her so dearly? These new regulations which treat all people alike, high or low, are all new to us. We cannot follow them all so soon! How can we suddenly change our habits of a lifetime in a few weeks? This is indeed most insulting to a noble family such as ours!'

13

After listening to all this, Usama felt inclined to agree with them. It was very harsh indeed to punish her like anyone else. They were of high birth. He promised he would try his best to convince the Blessed Prophet to let Fatima off leniently. 'Count on me', he said, 'I shall speak to the Prophet and do my best to save you and your daughter from disgrace.'

Usama waited until he found the Blessed Prophet alone; and then began his plea. 'Have you heard, O Messenger of Allah, about that poor lady who carries the same name

as your daughter, Fatima? She is accused of theft and faces punishment. This is indeed a terrible thing for any young woman, let alone a woman of high birth of the tribe of Makhzum! Surely there can be an exception in her case. Never has anyone in her family been punished for a crime.

'These standards of justice', continued Usama, 'are all new to the people of Makka, they have not yet learned that the rule of law is as much for a nobleman as for a common man. Wouldn't it be more prudent, and safer

O Believers, as witnesses to God,
Be firm in justice even against yourselves,
Even against your parents, or your relatives,
And whether it be against rich or poor.
Al-Nisā': 135

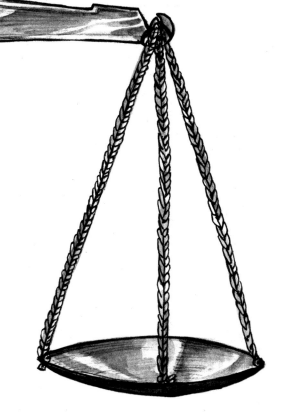

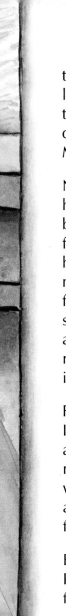

to mete out these punishments little by little, giving people time to adjust and thereby avoid the possibility of unrest and discontent among these newly converted Muslims?'

Now, as Usama was talking — as rapidly as he possibly could — the Blessed Prophet's back was turned to him, and yet he could feel the Blessed Prophet's displeasure at his words, and the longer he talked the more confused he became — the more he felt the wrongness of what he was saying, so that when the Blessed Prophet did turn around and face him he was so filled with repentance that he could but hang his head in shame.

Finally the Blessed Prophet spoke. 'Usama, I love you dearly, but think what you are asking me. You are asking me to relent, to refrain from carrying out a command which was given to me by Allah just because the accused person belongs to an upper-class family!'

By now, Usama was at the Blessed Prophet's feet, begging him to seek forgiveness from God for his mistake.

That night, after the evening Prayers, the Blessed Prophet stood up to address the congregation.

17

'*Allahu Akbar*', he began, 'many nations before you declined, weakened, and were ultimately destroyed only because of this fatal error: when someone who was highly placed committed a crime, he was let off, and when someone who was of humble stock committed the same crime, they punished him. I swear by the One in whose hands my life rests that even if Fatima, my daughter, had committed a theft, I would command that her hand be cut off.'

Such was the equality of justice practised and established by the Blessed Prophet and followed afterwards by many of those who ruled over their fellow Muslims, following in his footsteps.

2

You hypocrite!

'**A**mr was trembling with fury. 'You fool! You hypocrite!'

At these words a hush fell over the assembly and everyone held their breath with astonishment, so shocked were they at this accusation. Had 'Amr dared accuse al-Tajibi, this newly converted Muslim, of hypocrisy with nothing to justify it? 'Amr bin al'As had been a general, and was now the appointed governor of Egypt. In combat he had proved himself a great man, but he sometimes lost his temper and said things he did not mean. But in Islam hypocrisy is a great sin. To accuse a Muslim of hypocrisy was the worst of insults. It was a blight on his reputation.

The silence thickened as everyone listened for al-Tajibi's reply. His face was pale and his voice no more than a whisper as he turned to 'Amr. 'I swear by Allah and in front of these witnesses that since becoming a Muslim I have never committed an act of hypocrisy. I shall neither wash my head nor annoint it until I reach Umar and report to him the abuse which has been cast upon me here today.'

Al-Tajibi then left Egypt for Madina and after many days travel reached the Masjid al-Nabawi* where he joined in the Prayers, and then asked Umar for an audience. Al-Tajibi related the incident and the injustice done to him by 'Amr, and Umar lost no time in writing a letter.

'O 'Amr', it began, 'I have been told by al-Tajibi that you abused him and called him a hypocrite in public'. If you cannot support your accusation with two witnesses that al-Tajibi is indeed guilty of being a hypocrite, then you have committed an act of slander. In accordance with the law of Islam, he is entitled to punish you with forty lashes.'

Umar gave the letter to his envoy who accompanied al-Tajibi back to Egypt. Upon arriving at the Mosque in Egypt the two men waited until everyone had gathered, including 'Amr.

*The Mosque of the Blessed Prophet in Madina.

Then al-Tajibi stood up and spoke: 'I ask you all to bear witness that our governor, 'Amr bin al'As, without justification, slandered me by calling me a hypocrite in front of this assembly.'

Since everyone present had witnessed the accusation, they all stood up. Al-Tajibi then took the letter from Umar's envoy and handed it to 'Amr's secretary who read it aloud. When he came to the part about the punishment, 'Amr, 'Amr's secretary and his entourage became very upset. What was to happen now? Was a newly converted Muslim — a common Egyptian — going to whip the governor and conqueror of Egypt, a Chief from the noble tribe of the Quraysh?

'Amr's secretary came towards al-Tajibi with a smile. 'My dear brother, surely you don't really wish to whip your own governor? You must understand that 'Amr spoke thoughtlessly, in a moment of anger without meaning what he said. Certainly you are not a hypocrite. Allow us, then, to compensate you for your discomfort and humiliation. I assure you that we can be most generous…'

Al-Tajibi was too hurt and too angry to accept an apology. 'I do not wish to be compensated', he replied coldly. 'A houseful of gold will not make up for such an insult. I await 'Amr.'

At this the people began to lose patience. What was the matter with the man? 'Enough, al-Tajibi', they said. 'You are carrying this too far. Through his secretary 'Amr

23

apologises, and now you want to stage a ridiculous scene in public just to satisfy your ego. What is the use of that kind of revenge?'

All this time, 'Amr remained silent, seated with his men. Finally, it became clear to al-Tajibi that he was not going to obtain justice. 'I can see that none of you are prepared to uphold Umar's command', he said, and signalling to Umar's envoy, turned and left the mosque.

'Amr now began to reflect on his position. If al-Tajibi returned to Umar, then he, 'Amr, might be faced with even worse punishment. He stroked his beard in silence for a moment and then turned to one of his men. 'Call al-Tajibi and the envoy back here', he ordered.

When the two men returned, 'Amr stood up, removed his turban with great dignity, and kneeling down in front of al-Tajibi handed him his own whip. 'Strike then! 'Amr fears no man's lash and no man's ridicule', he stated.

The onlookers held their breath and stared in disbelief. What, was 'Amr, commander-in-chief, governor, victor, nobleman of the great clan of the Quraysh and Companion of the Blessed Prophet going to allow himself to be whipped by an insignificant Egyptian convert?

Al-Tajibi was not impressed by the scene. 'And now, O 'Amr', he asked, 'can all your authority, your power and your influence save you from your own mistakes?'

'Amr did not move an inch. 'Waste no more time. Do what you have been authorised to do', he answered.

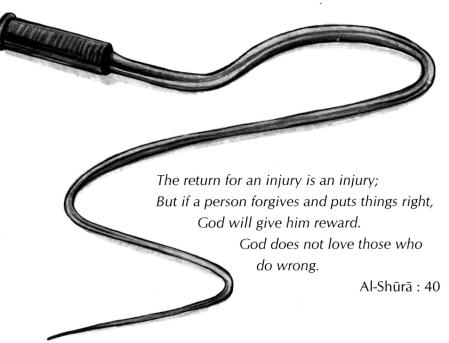

The return for an injury is an injury;
But if a person forgives and puts things right,
God will give him reward.
God does not love those who
do wrong.

Al-Shūrā : 40

Al-Tajibi stared for a moment at the figure kneeling in front of him, shook his head, and threw away the whip. 'I hereby forgive you, O 'Amr. I ask for no compensation. I only wish to show that in Islam, the honour and dignity of the most ordinary Muslim is as valuable and precious as that of a commander and chief, and a governor, such as you.'

And so saying, he left the mosque.

3

The proud son of a governor

U mar was sitting in the mosque one day when an
Egyptian entered and greeted him in the traditional
manner: 'As-Salamu'Alaykum — peace be with you', he
said and Umar replied, 'Wa'Alaykum as-Salam — and
with you'. The stranger then seated himself next to Umar
and addressed him as follows: 'If I present my case
before you, can I be certain that justice will be done and
protection granted?'

'Yes', replied Umar, 'I promise you both justice and protection. But tell me now, what is troubling you?'

The Egyptian began. 'Your governor in Egypt, 'Amr bin al'As, had the idea of holding a horse race. You know how we all love horses in Egypt, and as in Arabia, many of us own fine beasts. Everyone was eager to enter his horse in the race, and days were spent in preparation for what was to be a marvellous and very special event. I, myself, have a very beautiful and powerful mare, and I admit, I had every hope of winning.'

'Now, Muhammad, the son of 'Amr, also entered a fine
horse in the race. Well, the race began and each time the
horses came around in front of us we strained forward to
see who was in the lead. I could see that my own horse,
which had lagged behind at the start, was rapidly catching
up with the others and was even on its way past them as
they came around the second time. The third time around,
as the horses flew by where Muhammad was sitting, I
heard him cry out, 'My horse is in the lead! My horse
is winning!'

'Moments later they passed by me, and I saw clearly that it wasn't Muhammad's horse at all that was in the lead, but it was my horse that was winning. You can imagine how excited I became. Jumping up I began cheering and urging my horse on: by the Lord of Ka'ba, this is my mare which is leading! Suddenly Muhammad, with no warning at all, came at me with his whip and began lashing me as hard as he could. 'Take this, you commoner, take that! Remember, I'm the son of a nobleman and you're nothing but dirt!'

'Can you imagine, O *Amirul Muminin*,* what happened to me after that? I was thrown in prison... and all because 'Amr found out about the incident and was afraid I'd

*The Chief of the Believers.

come to you for protection and complain about his son's vile act. So there I lay in prison, and if it had not been for the kind understanding of one of the guards, who had heard the whole story, I would not be here asking for help.'

Upon hearing this story Umar fell silent. The only words he spoke were 'Sit down, brother. Stay with us'. Then Umar wrote a letter to the governor of Egypt ordering him to come immediately to Madina with his son Muhammad. The Egyptian was to remain until they arrived.

When 'Amr received this letter he was worried. He called his son and asked him what he had done. 'Have you committed a crime?' he asked.

'No, I swear', answered the youth.

'Then what does Umar want with both of us? You must have been up to something', said 'Amr shaking a finger at his son.

After a long journey, 'Amr and Muhammad arrived at the

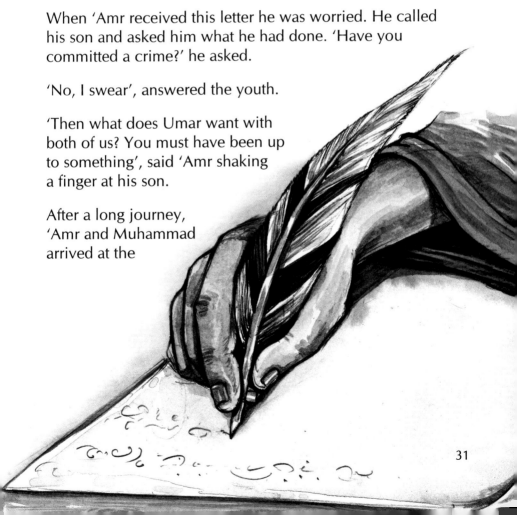

Masjid al-Nabawi in Madina. Crowds had
gathered, hearing that 'Amr was on his
way, and many of them cheered as the great
general strode past them and returned their
greeting. He was dressed in his usual splendid
garments and his proud young son walked behind him.

Umar wasted no time with formalities. 'Where is your
son', he asked abruptly. At this, Muhammad showed his
face from behind 'Amr's great cloak.

'Now, where is the Egyptian?'

'Here I am, *Amirul Muminin*.'

Umar handed him a whip. 'Now, Egyptian, lash that young son of a nobleman just as he whipped you!'

The Egyptian took the whip and administered several hard lashes. Umar nodded in approval, 'That's good... whip that son of a nobleman.'

After a while, the Egyptian stopped and Muhammad, humiliated and sore, scurried to the back of the crowd.

'And now!' said Umar, eyeing 'Amr with a piercing glance. 'And now, how about a few lashes for the

governor as well, since it is this governor whose power and authority has given the courage and the example to this son who considers himself superior to other men!'

'Amr's face turned pale at these words and the crowd held its breath, but the Egyptian shook his head. 'Amirul Muminin, I have had my revenge. 'Amr himself has done no wrong against me.'

'Very well', replied Umar. 'If you had wanted to whip the governor, as well, you would have had my permission. I would not have stopped you.'

Then he turned to 'Amr. 'These people are born free out of the wombs of their mothers. Since when have you turned them into your slaves?'

'Amr nodded and mumbled a few excuses. Umar then turned to the Egyptian.

'Go back to your land and live in peace and comfort. And if any wrong is committed against you, do not hesitate to let me know.'

The Egyptian thanked Umar profusely and the assembly returned to their homes having learned a lesson from the Caliph on equality before the law.

4

Innocent until proven guilty

In the days when Jarud was the governor of Bahrain there prevailed a state of emergency. The Muslims had been at war with the neighbouring empires and within the new territories which had been acquired by the Muslims, there remained a few inhabitants who were still rebelling against the new rule and against its leaders.

On a few occasions, Muslims had been betrayed by their own brothers who had gone over to the enemy through bribes and other forms of deceit. More than one battle had been lost because information had leaked out to the enemy.

37

Jarud, the governor, was very troubled by this and felt the need to tighten security and to be especially cautious. He demanded that any suspicious activity be reported to him immediately. One day some men from the area brought a fellow Muslim before Jarud. 'We have arrested this man because he was seen talking in private to a known enemy. There is no doubt that he was informing on us and intends to betray us', declared the men.

'What is your name?' asked Jarud sternly.

'You know very well, sir, my name is Idrias. I am a Muslim brother and I am innocent of these accusations.'

'If that is so, why were you talking to that man privately?'

'I happened to meet him on the way home. He began asking me questions. I told him I had nothing to say to him.'

40

'How do you expect me to believe that?' interrupted Jarud. 'For all I know you may already have betrayed us. This is no time for leniency and I cannot take any risks! Take this man away and execute him.'

As Idrias was led away to his execution, his cries of 'Umar, O Umar' resounded throughout the night.

It was not long before news of this execution came to the ears of Umar himself. Umar lost no time in sending for Jarud. When Jarud arrived in Madina he was escorted to Umar's quarters where he presented himself to the Caliph. Umar, upon seeing him grasped his spear in a symbolic gesture and called out 'Idrias, I hear you' three times before he turned to Jarud.

'I am awaiting your explanation for the execution of your Muslim brother, Idrias', he said.

'*Amirul Muminin*', began Jarud, 'You know what it is like in Bahrain at present. We are surrounded by enemies and a few spies from our own ranks who are divulging information. More than once we have been betrayed by men whom we thought trustworthy and faithful to the cause of Islam. They have proven to be weak and corruptible and have been the cause of many of our men losing their lives. In the case of Idrias, he was discovered conversing with the enemy. We could not afford the risk of betrayal.'

God commands justice and doing good;
And being generous towards fellow men;
He forbids indecency, injustice and insolence;
He instructs you that you may be reminded.

Naḥl: 90

'I ask you then', replied Umar in a cold voice, 'What proof did you have of his guilt?'

'No actual proof, *Amirul Muminin.*'

'So you admit that you executed this man on the grounds of mere *suspicion*?'

'That is correct, *Amirul Muminin.*'

Umar could restrain himself no longer. 'A man is never guilty of what he *intends* to do! If you had no proof of his guilt then he remained innocent! Never may a man be executed until proven guilty! Now I order you to pay retribution to his family and I hereby dismiss you from the post of governor of Bahrain', concluded Umar, turning his back on Jarud.

Umar's judgement thus made it clear to all Muslims that a man cannot be punished on the grounds of suspicion only, and that all Muslims are innocent until proven guilty.

5

Umar hears you!

The people of Madina remembered for a long time afterwards how Umar looked on that Friday morning when he came out of his house. They would remember always the pain and sadness in his eyes, his drawn face, and his voice moaning 'I hear you... I am coming, I am coming...' with his hands to his ears as if he were calling the *Azan*.

They stopped in their tracks as he went by. They whispered to one another asking what terrible thing could have befallen the Caliph. And when a man came out of Umar's house a short time after, they gathered around him asking for explanations. The man's face was grim as he told them what had happened.

That morning Umar had received the usual mail from the provinces and there was a letter about a certain governor — he did not care to mention which one — who was in command of an army some distance from his home. They were on a campaign headed East and had come to the banks of a river in an area which was unfamiliar to them. There were no boats in sight and there was no way they could judge the depth of the river. The governor had told them to seek out an inhabitant from the nearby village, which they did. They found an old man who could not give them the information they required, so the governor ordered him to get into the water and find out how deep it was. The old man protested, saying he was feeble and not able to stand extreme cold, but the governor insisted, and in the end the old man went into the water. He waded out until the water came up to his waist, then the current and the cold overwhelmed him and he began to drown. As he was drowning, he called out 'Umar, Umar, help me, help me!'

The people felt great sympathy for their Caliph. Indeed, this was difficult news for him to bear. No wonder he had been upset. Umar lost no time in issuing a command to the governor in question to report to Madina. The governor arrived in time for Prayers and afterwards went to greet Umar. But Umar did not return his greetings. In fact, Umar was so angry that he did not trust himself to speak. It wasn't until the seventh day after the governor arrived that Umar sent for him.

'Why did you send that man into the water to drown?' asked Umar, his face white and taut.

'I did not intend he should drown', explained the governor. 'I beg you to consider the circumstances. There was no boat, and no means of discovering the depth of the river. None of us knew the terrain, the currents or the probable depth and it was imperative that we reached the other side in order

47

48

to begin our siege before nightfall. It is usual practice to ask local inhabitants for help in such situations. I sent out for a villager, and this man was brought to me.'

Umar turned suddenly. 'An old man! A feeble old man who told you he could not survive the cold water!'

'That's right!' replied the governor, 'and neither would my men have survived! It is customary in times of war to sacrifice one man for the sake of many. Would you weigh the life of an old man, soon to die, against an army of the Faithful? May I remind you, Amirul Muminin, that we have conquered city after city, territory after territory...'

Umar was beside himself, 'Would you like to know how I would have it? I would have you killed as a punishment! If it were not for setting a precedent... Indeed! Who are the cities and the riches and the territories for? They are for the Muslim people! For the old men, the families and the poor as well as the soldiers and the statesmen! It is the ordinary Muslims like that old man who cried out for me in his final agony that I care about. I order you therefore, to compensate the old man's family and to get out of my sight. Never do I want to see your face around here again!'

At the governor's departure, Umar buried his head in his hands and prayed that Allah would forgive him for the mistakes and sins committed by the men under his rule.

Never should a Believer Kill a Believer;
But if it happens by mistake,
Compensation is due

Al-Nisa' : 92

6

The two garments

As soon as the people heard the *Azan* they hurried to the Mosque of the Prophet. The *Azan*, if not called to invite to one of the five daily Prayers, was a sign that they were invited to an important meeting to discuss some matter of public concern or to receive some urgent instructions.

51

This time Umar himself waited to address them. When the people had assembled, Umar rose and went and stood on the pulpit, from where he explained to the Muslims the task before them. Then he said, 'O people, listen to me. Allah will have mercy upon you!'

Suddenly a man from the congregation stood up. Everyone recognised him as Salman the Persian.

'We have listened but we shall not follow' he cried. 'We have listened but we shall not follow!'

Everyone was surprised. What was he talking about? Was it a sign of rebellion or indiscipline? Or did he have a complaint of some kind?

Umar remained calm and unruffled. He said, 'And why, O Salman, will you not follow?'

'You have not treated Muslims equally', Salman replied. 'You are not just. It seems that you have begun to lean towards worldly things. Only yesterday you distributed the garments that had come from Yemen. Everyone was given one garment but we find that

you yourself have two! You are Caliph, sure! But you are not entitled to take one garment more than what every other Muslim gets.'

Umar smiled and nodded. 'Where is my son, Abdullah?' he called. 'Will he stand up.'

Abdullah bin Umar stood up, 'I am here, *Amirul Muminin.*'

Umar turned towards him and said, 'To whom does this second garment belong? Will you explain?'

Abdullah said, 'Yes. This is my garment which I gave to my father.'

Umar then turned towards Salman and said, 'Salman, you were a little hasty in your judgement. I washed my clothes and they were wet. So I borrowed my son Abdullah's garment.'

Salman nodded and answered 'Now you may speak freely. We shall listen and we shall obey.'

Umar ruled over a kingdom which extended as far as
Egypt. Yet he was accountable to the people for each
single item which might be found in his possession above
what was given to any ordinary Muslim. The people
were bold enough to ask questions, to bring the Caliph to
account, and even refuse to obey him.

7

The hard-hearted governor

One day Umar was seated in his house in Madina awaiting the arrival of two tribal chiefs who had been recommended to him for the post of governor. It was not easy to choose a man to be governor. Even if he was known to be an adept and intelligent leader, it was not always certain he would be humane and compassionate as well.

The first candidate to arrive was most impressive. 'Peace be with you and may the mercy and blessings of Allah fall upon you', he announced in beautiful Arabic with a flourish of his hand. Umar noted that he had the bearing of a king and was impeccably dressed in a handsomely stitched garment and a magnificent turban. Umar invited him to sit, which he did without hesitation, on the mat next to Umar, and helped himself to some dates which had been placed there for guests. After a few words with the man, Umar was convinced he must be an able and intelligent leader, perfectly suited for the governorship.

After a while, their conversation was abruptly interrupted by the second candidate who entered in a terrible hurry, apologising for his lateness, and all the while brushing the dust off his shabby garment and adjusting his turban which had slipped slightly over one ear. 'Oh *Amirul Muminin*, pardon me for being late. You see, on my way here I came across an old woman and her donkey. The donkey's foot was caught between two rocks... I couldn't pass by without helping her... It was a tough job, I tell you... so I'm afraid I'm a little late.'

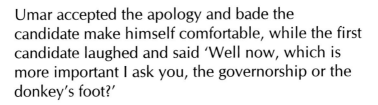

Umar accepted the apology and bade the candidate make himself comfortable, while the first candidate laughed and said 'Well now, which is more important I ask you, the governorship or the donkey's foot?'

At this moment one of Umar's children ran into the room and jumped on Umar's lap. Umar cuddled the child in his arms and gave him two big kisses on the head.

The first candidate could not hide his astonishment and displeasure at such a sight. 'Never have I done such a thing, *Amirul Muminin*. My ten children do not even dare come *near* me, and I would certainly never kiss them.'

Umar took a long look at the man and shook his head, 'Well, there's not much I can do about that. If Allah has drained your heart of kindness, then so be it. But remember that Allah shows mercy only to those who are merciful towards His creatures.'

Umar noticed that the second candidate was looking a bit bashful and ashamed and asked him what was the matter.

'Well you see, *Amirul Muminin*, I have the opposite trouble', confessed the man. 'I have only five children but they are always jumping all over me. Before I left, the littlest one, Laila is her name, didn't want me to go... she kept clinging to my robe and wanting me to take her, which is why, you see, my garment is a little soiled.'

Umar smiled and looked towards his secretary who was waiting to hear which man Umar had decided upon. 'Please write this second candidate a letter of appointment to the governorship, I believe he is the right man for the job.'

The first candidate, upon hearing Umar's decision, was taken with a sudden fit of coughing.

'You see', explained Umar to the first candidate, 'It is not enough to be a leader and a proud man. A tribal chief who becomes governor must also have compassion and must wish to take the time to help others. And this good man, since he has been here, has given me proof of both qualities.'

The first candidate, who had managed to stop coughing, tried hard to understand what Umar was talking about, but since Allah had hardened his heart to such matters, he left without understanding why he had lost the governorship to an untidy man who concerned himself with children, donkeys and old women.